WORLD OF ENGINEERING

BUILDING A SHIP

NATALIE HUMPHREY

PowerKiDS press

Published in 2024 by The Rosen Publishing Group, Inc.
2544 Clinton Street, Buffalo, NY 14224

Portions of this work were originally authored by Sam Aloian and published as *How a Ship Is Built.* All new material in this edition was authored by Natalie Humphrey.

Editor: Natalie Humphrey
Designer: Rachel Rising

Photo Credits: Cover, Rudmer Zwerver/Shutterstock.com; Cover, pp. 1-24 Alef-Beth/Shutterstock.com; Cover, pp. 1-24 Artistdesign29/Shutterstock.com; Cover, pp. 1, 3, 22-24 RoseRodionova/Shutterstock.com; Cover, p. 1 Creative Hawk/Shutterstock.com; p. 5 https://commons.wikimedia.org/wiki/File:Drents_Museum_prehistoric_8943.jpg; p. 7 TarikVision/Shutterstock.com; p. 9 Nanisimova/Shutterstock.com; p. 10 Ljupco Smokovski/Shutterstock.com; p. 11 Fouad A. Saad/Shutterstock.com; p. 13 Khrushchev Georgy/Shutterstock.com; p. 15 Studio 37/Shutterstock.com; p. 16 Aun Photographer/Shutterstock.com; p. 17 Bogdan VASILESCU/Shutterstock.com; p. 19 Igor Hotinsky/Shutterstock.com; p. 20 APRIORI vector design/Shutterstock.com; p. 20 noir_illustration/Shutterstock.com; p. 21 VectorArtist7/Shutterstock.com; p. 21 Macrovector/Shutterstock.com; p. 21 AmazeinDesign/Shutterstock.com; p. 21 kvector/Shutterstock.com.

Author: Humphrey, Natalie.
Title: Building a ship / Natalie Humphrey.
Description: Buffalo, New York : Powerkids Press, 2024. | Series: World of engineering | Includes index, glossary, and bibliographic information
Identifiers: ISBN 9781642826494 (pbk) | ISBN 9781642826500 (library bound) | ISBN 9781642826517 (ebook)
Subjects: LCSH: Boatbuilding-- Juvenile literature | Engineering--Juvenile literature
Classification: LCC VM298.5 H86 2024 | DDC 623.8--dc24

Manufactured in the United States of America

CPSIA Compliance Information: Batch #CSPK24. For Further Information contact Rosen Publishing at 1-800-237-9932.

CONTENTS

SETTING SAIL

Throughout history, boats have helped people get from place to place. Some boats are small and only meant for one or two people. Other boats are big enough to carry hundreds of people at the same time!

From military ships big enough for airplanes to land on, to cargo ships that move goods from place to place, ships are an important part of our world today. But what goes in to building a ship? Let's find out!

ENGINEERING WONDERS

Is it a boat? Or a ship? Boats are a smaller form of ship. Ships can be very large and travel in deeper water.

THE OLDEST KNOWN BOAT IS THE PESSE **CANOE** FROM AROUND 8,000 BCE!

All boats need to be able to do one thing: float! The ability to float in water is called buoyancy. When a boat is put in water it displaces, or takes the place of, an amount of water equal to its weight.

Boats float when they're less **dense** than the water they're in. The weight of the water also puts **pressure** on the sides of the boat. This means that boats need to be made of **materials** that are strong without being too dense.

ENGINEERING WONDERS

If there's a crack in the boat's hull, or the outer walls of the boat, it may cause the boat to sink!

BOATS MADE OUT OF METAL TAKE A LOT OF ENGINEERING TO FLOAT!

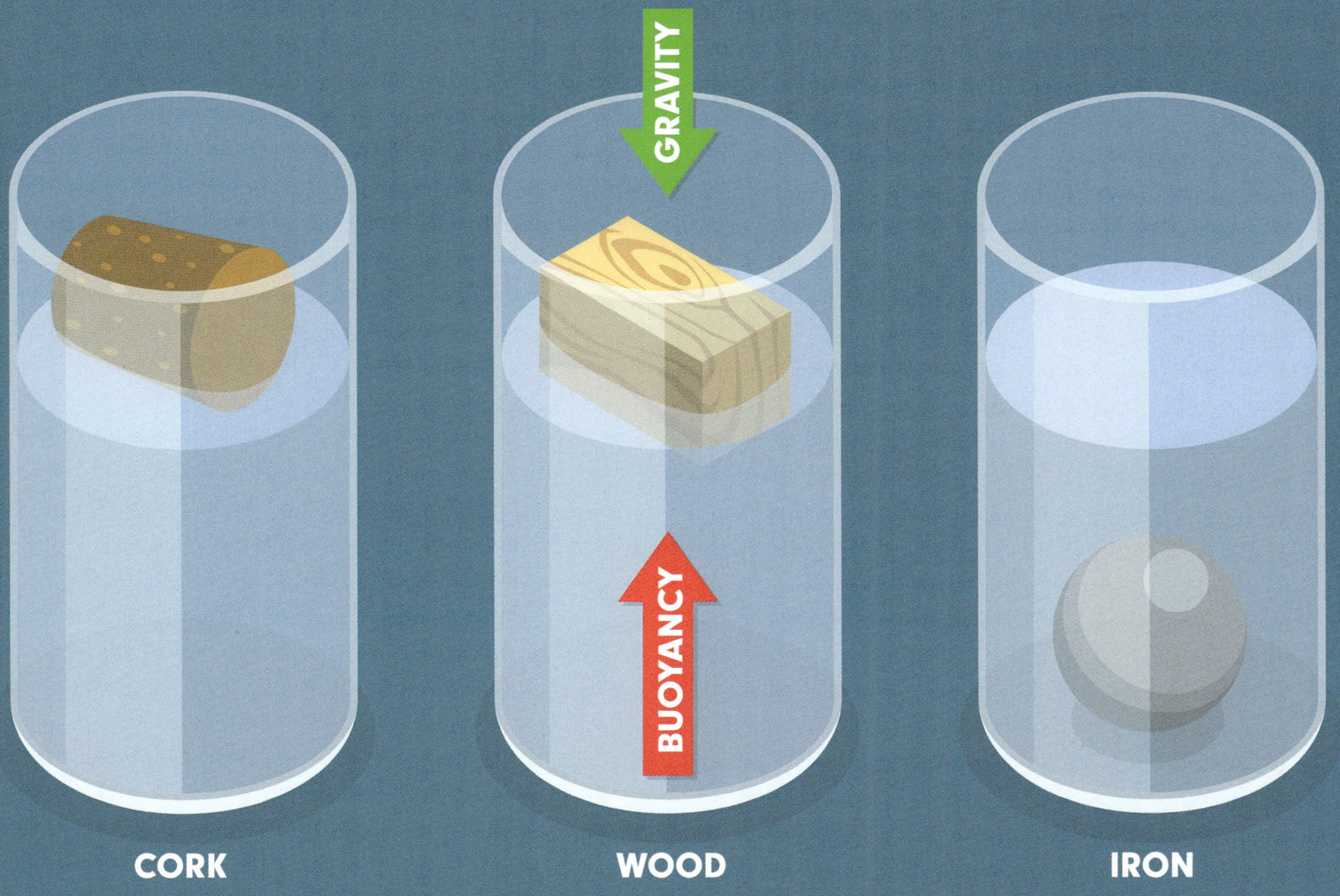

BUILDING A BOAT

Early boats were made from wood. Wood often floats naturally and is light and strong. Pieces of wood were fitted together to make them watertight to stop leaks that could sink the boat. Early boats often moved using sails to catch the wind. They also used paddles, which people rowed in the water to make the boat move.

By studying the science of how boats float and how they move in water, shipbuilders have been able to improve boats. Newer boats are much larger and faster than the first boats.

ENGINEERING WONDERS

Naval architects and marine engineers are people who **design** large ships. They also build and keep ships in shape.

SOME SMALLER BOATS ARE STILL MADE FROM WOOD TODAY, BUT LARGER BOATS ARE USUALLY MADE OF OTHER MATERIALS.

MAKING METAL FLOAT

There are a lot of tricks that shipbuilders use to design large ships. To make sure bigger ships are buoyant, builders make their hulls from two pieces of metal. These pieces are filled with air. The steel hull is heavy and strong, but the air is much lighter than water.

Naval architects work to make sure ships won't capsize, or tip over. Flat-bottomed boats are more **stable** in water. Ships that are more pointed can move easier through the water.

ENGINEERING WONDERS

Hydrokinetics is the study of how **fluids**, such as water, move. Naval architects study hydrokinetics to help them understand how the boats will move through the water.

NAVAL ARCHITECTS NEED TO LOOK AT WHAT THE BOAT WILL BE USED FOR TO PICK THE RIGHT HULL SHAPE FOR THE JOB.

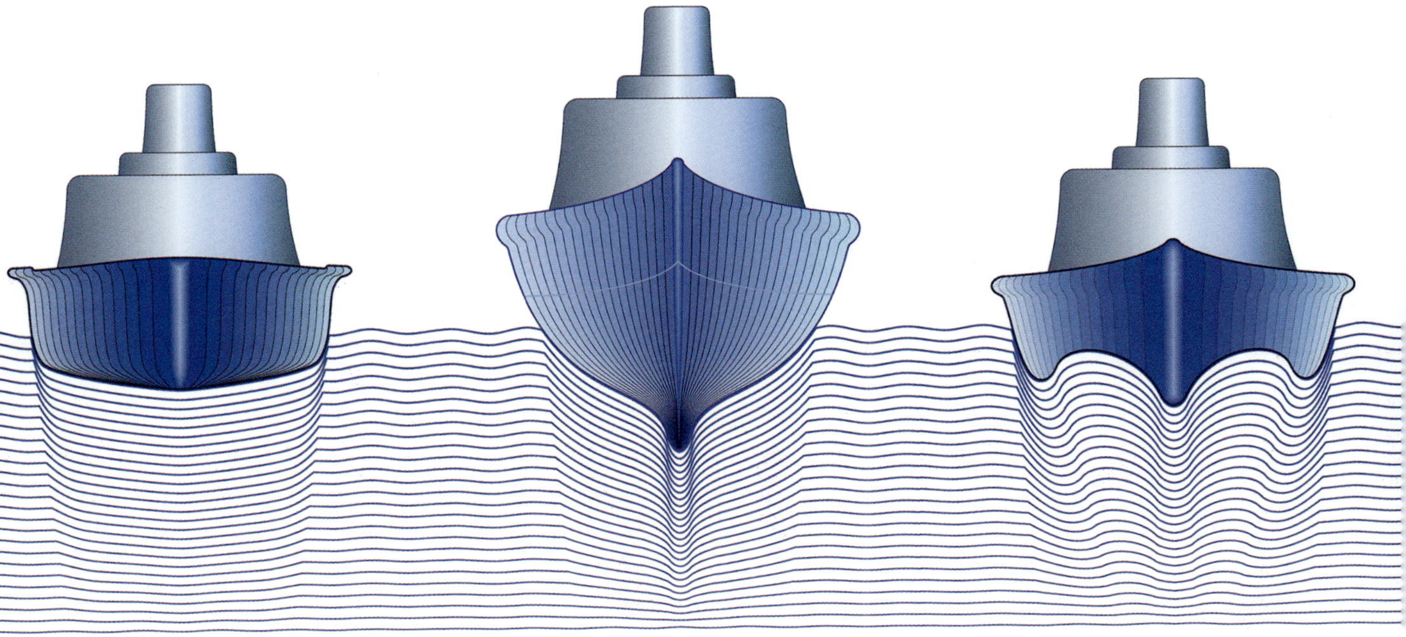

FLAT

ROUND WITH KEEL

MULTI HULLED

After the naval architects finish creating the design for the ship, shipbuilders make sure they have the right materials and workers for the job. Ships are built in a shipyard. While shipyards are built near water, smaller ships start life on land. Larger ships are built at a **dry dock**.

The keel, or the main backbone of the ship's hull, is built first. Builders put together large pieces of metal and bring them to the dry dock. They then **weld** the pieces to form the hull.

ENGINEERING WONDERS

During construction, workers use tall wooden or concrete pieces called ways to hold up the ship's hull. Concrete is a mix of water, stone, sand, and soft grey powder that becomes hard and strong when it's dry.

TO BUILD LARGE SHIPS, STEELWORKERS, WELDERS, AND OTHER SPECIALIZED WORKERS ARE NEEDED.

LAUNCHING THE SHIP

Once workers finish building the hull, they usually **launch** the incomplete ship into the water. They launch some small ships sideways and large ships from the bow (front) to the stern (back). Cables, ropes, or chains help keep the hull steady as workers carefully move the ship into the water to test its buoyancy.

For dry dock-built ships, workers flood the docks to test for leaks in the hull. Once all the tests are finished and workers know the ship is buoyant, construction starts on the inside of the ship.

ENGINEERING WONDERS

To help design the ship before construction starts, shipbuilders usually make a lines plan. A lines plan is a small-scale drawing of a ship.

DRY DOCKS CAN ALSO BE USED IF A SHIP NEEDS REPAIRS, OR TO BE FIXED.

Workers put in the ship's engine. They also connect the ships steering systems. The steering systems help the ship's captain control which direction the ship will go in. Workers put in ropes and chains called rigging. They also add decks or flooring that cover the lower levels of the ship.

Workers often build ships in sections to make the construction process easier. When the ship is complete, they clean, paint, and dock it to get ready for the final step in construction.

ENGINEERING WONDERS

Many ships also have rooms, beds, and bathrooms. This is so everyone can feel comfortable on board the ship.

SHIPBUILDERS USE SPECIAL KINDS OF PAINT THAT KEEP THE SHIP SAFE FROM RUSTING.

THE SEA TRIALS

Before a ship is ready for use, it must go through many sea trials, or tests in the water. These trials make sure a ship is seaworthy, or ready for its job. Naval architects test everything on board the ship, from the ship's **anchor** to the its engines. They will also test the ship's speed and how **maneuverable** it is in the water.

Even if a ship passes its sea trials, many are tested each time they return to shore!

ENGINEERING WONDERS

Military ships, such as aircraft carriers, also have their weapons tested during the sea trials.

ENGINEERS CAN USE SPECIAL TOOLS TO CHECK FOR LEAKS ON A SHIP.

MAKE YOUR OWN BOAT

Now that you know how ships and boats are built, it's time to make your own. Here's what you need to make your own boat!

WHAT YOU NEED

- crayon
- paper
- scissors
- straw
- tape

HOW TO

1. Draw the shape of your ship's hull and sail on paper.
2. Carefully cut out your shapes using scissors. (Ask an adult for help!)
3. Fold the hull into shape following the dotted lines.
4. Tape hull together.
5. Make sure your boat is watertight using tape to cover any holes.
6. Tape your sail to the straw.
7. Tape sail to hull.
8. Set sail with your new boat!

GLOSSARY

anchor: A heavy object or device that holds a boat in one place.

canoe: A small boat that's pointed at both ends and is usually moved by a paddle.

dense: Lots of matter packed close together in a small area.

design: To create a plan for something.

dry dock: A dock without water used for the building or fixing of ships.

fluid: A substance that flows freely like water.

launch: To officially start something.

maneuverable: Able to change position easily.

material: Something from which something else can be made.

pressure: A force that pushes on something else.

stable: Not likely to change suddenly or greatly.

weld: To join two pieces of metal together by melting them.

FOR MORE INFORMATION

BOOKS

Ventura, Marne. *Building a Boat that Floats*. North Mankato, MN: Pebble, 2020.

Washburne, Sophie. *Great Ship Designs*. New York, NY: Cavendish Square Publishing, 2023.

WEBSITES

Science Kids
www.sciencekids.co.nz/sciencefacts/vehicles/boats.html
Learn more about different kinds of boats and how they work.

Wonderopolis
www.wonderopolis.org/wonder/how-do-boats-float
Learn more about how boats and other things float in water.

Publisher's note to educators and parents: Our editors have carefully reviewed these websites to ensure that they are suitable for students. Many websites change frequently, however, and we cannot guarantee that a site's future contents will continue to meet our high standards of quality and educational value. Be advised that students should be closely supervised whenever they access the internet.

INDEX